BRITAIN IN PICTURES
THE BRITISH PEOPLE IN PICTURES

ISLANDS
ROUND BRITAIN

GENERAL EDITOR
W. J. TURNER

The Editor is most grateful to all those who have
so kindly helped in the selection of illustrations
especially to officials of the various public
Museums Libraries and Galleries and
to all others who have generously
allowed pictures and MSS
to be reproduced

ISLANDS
ROUND BRITAIN

R. M. LOCKLEY

WITH
8 PLATES IN COLOUR
AND
27 ILLUSTRATIONS IN
BLACK & WHITE

COLLINS · 14 ST. JAMES'S PLACE · LONDON
MCMXLVI

PRODUCED BY
ADPRINT LIMITED LONDON

FIRST PUBLISHED   1945
SECOND IMPRESSION 1946

PRINTED IN GREAT BRITAIN BY
CLARKE & SHERWELL LTD NORTHAMPTON
ON MELLOTEX BOOK PAPER MADE BY
TULLIS RUSSELL & CO LTD MARKINCH SCOTLAND

Quinboro Castle, in the Ile of Shepy

LIST OF ILLUSTRATIONS

PLATES IN COLOUR

THE ISLE OF ANGLESEY, THE ISLE OF MAN, AND THE ISLE OF WIGHT
Coloured engraving of three maps by Johann Blaeu, 1650

SHANKLIN, ISLE OF WIGHT
Water colour by Peter de Wint, 1784-1849

HOLY ISLAND
Water colour by John Varley, 1778-1842

GENERAL VIEW OF GUERNSEY FROM PORT GEORGE
Water colour by R. P. Leitch c. 1850

ST. HELIER, JERSEY
Water colour by J. Young

A VIEW OF THE BAY AND PIER OF DOUGLAS, ISLE OF MAN
Coloured engraving by J. Burman

THE ISLE OF STAFFA
Water colour by Copley Fielding, 1787-1855

SCOOR EIG, ISLE OF EIG
Coloured aquatint by William Daniell
From Richard Ayton's *A Voyage Round Great Britain*, 1813

BLACK AND WHITE ILLUSTRATIONS

PAGE

QUEENSBOROUGH CASTLE IN THE ISLE OF
SHEPPEY   5
Engraving by Wenceslaus Hollar
By gracious permission of H.M. The King

ST. CUTHBERT IN HIS CURRAGH   7
Illumination from Bede's *Life and Miracles
of St. Cuthbert*. Late twelfth century Ms.
By courtesy of the Trustees of the British Museum

BIRDS BREAKFASTING, MULL   9
Drawing by H. D. Graham, 1852, from
The Birds of Iona and Mull, 1890

ST. CUTHBERT'S DUCK   10
Wood engraving by Thomas Bewick,
from his *British Birds*, 1804

HOLY ISLAND CATHEDRAL   11
Drawing by J. M. W. Turner engraved by
C. Turner, 1808. From Turner's *Liber
Studiorum*

SEAL   12
Engraving from the English edition of
the Comte de Buffon's *Natural History*,
1812

SMALL SEAL   13
Engraving from the English edition of the
Comte de Buffon's *Natural History*, 1812

MAP OF THE BRITISH ISLES SHOWING THE
CHIEF PLACES MENTIONED IN THE TEXT   15

ST. MARY, SCILLY ISLES   16
Water colour by J. C. Schetky
By gracious permission of H.M. The King

ST. MICHAEL'S MOUNT   17
Engraving from *England Delineated*, 1804

ST. CATHERINE'S BAY, ST. MARTIN'S,
JERSEY   19
Coloured lithograph by P. J. Ouless, 1842
By courtesy of the Parker Gallery, London

BLACK MARBLE QUARRY NEAR RED WHARF
BAY, ANGLESEY   20
Drawn and engraved by William Daniell
from Ayton's *A Voyage Round Great
Britain*, 1813

GANNET   23
Painting by Edwards engraved by R.
Murray from T. Pennant's *A Tour in
Scotland*, 1799

ROPE BRIDGE NEAR THE LIGHTHOUSE,
HOLY HEAD   26
Drawn and engraved by William Daniell
from Ayton's *A Voyage Round Great
Britain*, 1813

PUFFIN ISLAND, ANGLESEY   27
Drawn and engraved by William Daniell
from Ayton's *A Voyage Round Great
Britain*, 1813

THE CATHEDRAL, ISLE OF MAN   28
Seventeenth century engraving
By courtesy of the Trustees of the British Museum

LOCH SCAVIG, ISLE OF SKYE   29
Drawn and engraved by William Daniell
from Ayton's *A Voyage Round Great
Britain*, 1813

CIRCLE OF STONES AT TURMORE, ISLE OF
ARRAN   30
Water colour by W. A. Nesfield, 1793-1881
By courtesy of the Victoria & Albert Museum

THE BASS ROCK   31
Drawing by J. M. W. Turner engraved by
W. Millar

INTERIOR OF A FOULA COTTAGE   35
Woodcut from Kirkwell's *Handbook to
the Shetland Islands*, 1878

IONA CATHEDRAL   37
Engraving by Joseph Skelton from the
Guide Pittoresque du Voyageur en Ecosse,
Paris, 1838

WRECK OF THE 'LESSING,'—FAIR ISLE   38
Woodcut from Kirkwell's *Handbook to
the Shetland Islands*

DRONGS IN THE BAY OF ST. MAGNUS   39
Engraving by C. Thomson from S. Hib-
bert's *Description of the Shetland Islands*,
1822

DOON POINT, RATHLIN   43
Water colour by A. Nicholl engraved by
S. G. Hughes, 1835, from *Picturesque
Sketches of . . . the Coast Scenery of
Ireland*

STORMY PETREL   44
Engraving from the English edition of the
Comte de Buffon's *Natural History*, 1812

DUN AENGUS IN THE ISLE OF ARAN   47
Engraving from F. Grose's *The Antiquities
of Ireland*, 1795

SCUDDING HOME   48
Drawing by H. G. Graham from *The
Birds of Iona and Mull*, 1890

O these endless little isles . . .
lying clad with soft verdure,
and in thine awful solitude,
afar off in the lap of wild ocean,—
not to see thee with the carnal eye,
will be to have seen nothing! T. S. MUIR

INTRODUCTION

HOW MANY ISLANDS ARE THERE ROUND THE coasts of Britain? Surely it is part of my duty, in writing this book, to give an approximate figure? Or shall I agree with the old belief according to which there are as many islands round England as there are hours in the day, round Wales as there are months in the year, round Ireland as there are weeks in the year and round Scotland as there are days in the year: a total of 453?

It is certainly correct to say that there are 453 islands conforming to a certain acreage. But so much depends on your definition of an island. There are far more than 453 if we accept every piece of grass-grown land surrounded by the sea. After all the merest rock containing only one sea-bird's nest and a lighthouse is an island, according to the text-books on geography. Thus the main mass of England-Wales-Scotland, commonly referred to as Great Britain, is an island (though it contains something like forty million inhabitants) equally with the Eddystone Lighthouse containing three keepers.

Ireland, with its Southern and Northern factions, is the next largest island in these Isles. Then there is the Isle of Man, the Isle of Wight, Anglesey, Skye—to say nothing of such large islands as Mull, Islay, Arran in the Clyde and Aran off Galway and Aran off Donegal. Or such large groups or archipelagos as the Shetlands, the Orkneys and the Outer and Inner Hebrides.

But upon these larger islands and groups as such it is not my intention to dwell extensively here. Their history and topography is already overwritten. This book is intended rather to describe some of the more interesting small islands which are as yet little known, but which catch the imagination with their suggestion of remote charm, and their unspoilt human and natural ecology or associations.

There is something about a small island that satisfies the heart of man. "Ah, if only that little island were mine. What fun I could have with it!" we say. And we plan what we could do with a little kingdom of our own set in the silver sea. So much we could do, and no one would say us nay! We should build our little house out of driftwood—or pine tree logs if any were handy to cut; rear a family of joyous sturdy children—or turn hermit if our philo-progenitiveness were weak; our amateur engineering and constructive ingenuity would have a gloriously free field for development—or we could merely laze in the sun and live on the wild fruits: depending on the climate and customs and natural fertility of the island of our dreams.

Generally however the islands of Britain do not lend themselves to the lazy idyllic life of perpetual sunshine, of warm seas full of fish, and fruit hanging from every tree and bush. The North Atlantic climate provides instead perpetual breezes interspersed with heavy westerly gales and intermittent sunshine. The fruits of our cold earth and sea are only won by diligence with cultivator's tools and fisherman's net and line.

Nevertheless this general specification of our small British islands has a good deal to commend it to our notice, and there are very few, and of the really attractive almost none, to-day which are not occupied by moderately happy owners, tenants, "exploiters," lighthouse-keepers, coastguards and/ or, best of all, genuine native farmers and fishermen.

Let me explain the rather unpopular term "exploiters." All of us, directly or indirectly, are exploiters, whether we get our living by dividends exploited for us by the money-shufflers in cities, or by exploiting the demand for food by farming, or by fishing, or by hotel-keeping, or by catering for the universal love of reading by writing. It is however common to use the word in a derogatory sense to describe those who put up or keep hotels and boarding-houses on lovely remote islands, and so provide a good deal of happiness for many who could not otherwise visit the islands. But provided the architecture and lay-out fits the environment, the idea is sound. Those who poke names at these proprietors of houses of accommodation on islands are generally persons with private means, or they may be famous authors, or merely grumpy hermits, who prefer to keep their houses and islands strictly for their own enjoyment; justifiably where the island is a tiny one, but often wrongly where the island is so large that the owner-occupier himself has never become intimately acquainted with every part thereof.

In our tour we shall find every sort of exploiter in possession of the little islands, from the peasant-fisherman struggling with adversity or enjoying a moderate prosperity to the squire in his island castle. It will be for the reader to judge whether their occupation and stewardship is good or bad, and what, if anything, can be done in a world thirsting to be planned, to better the situation.

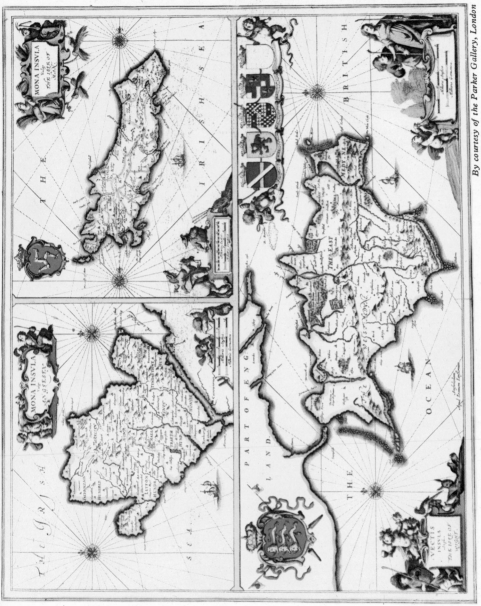

THE ISLE OF ANGLESEY, THE ISLE OF MAN, AND THE ISLE OF WIGHT

Coloured engraving of three maps by Johann Blaeu, 1650

71

SHANKLIN, ISLE OF WIGHT

Water colour by Peter de Wint, 1784-1849

BIRDS BREAKFASTING, MULL
Drawing by H. D. Graham, 1852

THE ISLANDS OF ENGLAND

THE Isle of Wight is England's largest island. For those who like a large and comfortable island home, and the greatest possible variety of moor, down, wood and farm land, Wight provides all within her lovely white cliffs, sandy bays, sheltered roadsteads and exposed headlands: all indeed that is miniature of the yeoman England loved by Englishmen. Her clean neat villages are linked by good roads, and the whole island may be skimmed in two days of quiet motoring. Wight is the bastion which makes and protects the waterway of the Solent and the harbours of Southampton and Portsmouth, with their tradition of great ocean-going merchant ships and warships. Wight draws thousands of holiday makers, but hundreds who work in Southampton, Gosport and Portsmouth also contrive to live on the island, in its little north side towns of Newport, Cowes and Ryde, using the excellent ferry services to transport them from their offices on the "mainland."

There are no other large islands off the English coast. If we start at the most northern tip, where the Tweed divides England from Scotland, and work southwards, there are first the Northumbrian islands of Holy Island, the Farnes group and Coquet: a nondescript collection, for Holy Island can be reached by a horse and cart at low tide, the Farnes are little more than a collection of small rocks and Coquet is but ten acres in extent.

All these islands are associated with sea-birds and men of prayer. The gentle St. Cuthbert had his headquarters here and so fond was he of the sea-birds that he gave his name to the eider-duck. "St. Cuthbert's ducks" followed him through the small islands and nested wherever he had trod,

9

it is said. Even to-day the eider-duck does not nest farther south than Coquet.

Holy Isle with its cathedral became a place of pilgrimage for the admirers of St. Cuthbert, but it is said that the saint loved Coquet best, and, escaping the notoriety and busy life of the people of Holy Isle, he would slip over to the little island for the sake of a week-end of peace and prayer in his cell there. Here he was inaccessible as long as the seas roared over the shallow reefs which surround Coquet. In Warkworth Church on the mainland opposite there is a very old wood relief of St. Cuthbert embarking for Coquet in A.D. 684. Prayers said on Coquet were supposed to be more than usually efficacious. In 1091, the monks of Coquet by diligent prayer are said to have wrecked the ships of the Scottish expedition of William Rufus. To-day the remains of the monks' cells are incorporated in the lighthouse buildings, which were built to accommodate three keepers and their families. The island was very fertile, its ten acres once supporting three cows and large gardens. The wives and families are now banished to the mainland, and some fifty pairs of St. Cuthbert's ducks make it their home. It is a great halting place for migratory birds, of which the woodcock is first favourite with the lighthouse-keepers and for a very sensible reason!

The Farne Islands consist of seven principal islets, and numerous rocks and skerries besides. Each of the seven has its special attraction. The Inner Farne, with its flower-filled grassy slope, was St. Cuthbert's favourite. Here he had a cell, the site of which is now occupied by a restored chapel. In keeping with the tradition it is here that the docile "Cuddy-ducks" breed in greatest number.

ST. CUTHBERT'S DUCK
Wood engraving by Bewick, 1804

10

HOLY ISLAND CATHEDRAL
Drawing by J. M. W. Turner engraved by C. Turner, 1808

Best known of the Farnes is the Longstone, with its lighthouse, scene of the heroic exploit of Grace Darling, so well-known that it was a surprise to me to find its authenticity doubted locally. "A prophet is not without honour save in his own country." But there is no doubt whatsoever that Grace and her father effected the rescue of the wrecked sailors; some say that the terrible ordeal resulted in the death of Grace early in life. The name Darling still survives round about Seahouses on the mainland opposite and until recently a relative of Grace's was a bird-watcher on the Inner Farne.

The Brownsman is the home of a colony of the charming kittiwake gull, the smallest, and from the human standpoint, the most quiet, inoffensive and dove-like of all the gulls. One kittiwake, ringed on the Brownsman on July 29, 1929, was subsequently caught on board ship the *Arctic Queen* in Davis Strait, West Greenland, so providing the opening evidence of a migration long suspected, and since confirmed by other British-ringed kittiwakes recovered in America.

The Pinnacles are the most astonishing islets of the Farnes, standing perpendicularly, their flat-topped basalt tables covered with communally-nesting guillemots, the water around crowded with the mates of these birds, which dive with half-open wings as your boat approaches. A perpetual groaning goes up from the slum-like loomery, while other strange bird-noises come from the Megstone Rock, the special home of the cormorant. Terns, herring and black-backed gulls, puffins, razorbills, oyster-catchers, and of late increasing numbers of fulmar petrels—all these, too, nest on the Farnes, making for the lover of birds on a visit in summer an exciting and long-to-be-remembered scene. While for those who can make the journey in early autumn, after the sea-birds have flown, and the bright sea-flowers have turned to seed, there are the calves of the grey (or Atlantic) seals to be visited. At this quiet season, just before the equinoctial gales, the cow seals search out some cave or rocky corner above high tide and there drop their white-coated baby. This remains on shore for about six weeks, being suckled and protected by the cow. During this period the white fur is moulted for the first coat of dappled grey.

The Farne Islands have been secured by the National Trust, which has placed their management in the hands of a local Farne Islands Association, whose principal duty is to see that the status quo of rich sea-bird and maritime life is maintained. This policy has been successful.

Follow the coast southward. There is no true island left on the North Sea coast of England. Parts of the Norfolk, Suffolk, Essex, and Kent coasts become enisled at high tide. The so-called islands of Mersea, Canvey, Sheppey, and Thanet carry bridges and are heavily populated. Nor is there any small island worthy of the name throughout the English Channel until we reach the Isles of Scilly.

Mention must be made, however, of the "High-water-only" Norfolk island of Scolt Head, reached by ferry from Brancaster. It became famous in a night when the late E. L. Turner offered to be the first watcher when the National Trust acquired the island, and declared it a sanctuary for wild life in

SEAL
Engraving from Buffon's *Natural History*, 1812

12

1923. Miss Turner was described at once as the "Loneliest Woman in England." But having a fund of inward cheerfulness and plenty to do, she found her solitude in the little watcher's hut set in the dunes and the marram-grass and the linnet-haunted sueda bushes anything but lonely. Publicity brought visitors by almost every tide, and skilfully she used them, as all wise islanders should, to fetch and carry water and driftwood, and to stand watch over the colonies of sea-swallows. All this is told in her delightful book *Scolt Head*, which describes the great autumn and spring migrations which pass through the island, and the nesting colonies of common, little, Sandwich and roseate terns which she guarded.

Scolt Head, like the Farnes, is an excellent example of what can be done by public effort in the permanent acquisition and maintenance of an island sanctu-

SMALL SEAL
Engraving from Buffon's *Natural History*, 1812

ary where varied forms of wild life, both plant and animal, can be intelligently studied and preserved. Research on tide-movements and coast erosion has also been carried out. The Norfolk and Norwich Naturalists Society, as the most interested and capable local body, is responsible to the National Trust for the supervision of this nation-owned Nature Reserve.

From the sand-dunes and dry east winds and late summer of the North Sea to the mild wet west winds and early spring flowers of Cornwall is a long leap. Yet much of the wild life of the Isles of Scilly is akin to that of the Farnes—the same quantities of sea-birds and seals, inhabiting islands with somewhat different names: Annet, Mincarlo, Illiswilgig, the Western and Eastern Rocks. There are shearwaters and petrels nesting in the Scillies, too, the first of many which breed only on the west side of Britain.

But "the Isles of Scilly" (as the islanders prefer to designate them in preference to "the Scillies" or "Scilly Isles") are more remarkable for their prosperous communities of small farmers, the descendants, as legend tells

13

us, of the inhabitants of the Lost Land of Lyonesse, a great and fair country that once united the Isles with the mainland of Cornwall. The remnants of King Arthur's Knights, after the death of their King in his last great battle, fled across Lyonesse; a great storm followed them and the sea buried his enemy Mordred and Mordred's pursuing company, leaving the Knights safe on the granite shores of the five inhabited islands and their two hundred satellite islets and rocks, grouped together about twenty-eight miles from the Land's End.

The prosperity now enjoyed by the Scillonians is not an old one—theirs is a stormy and grim history. In Roman times the Isles were a place of banishment for heretics. In A.D. 384 the Bishops Instantius and Tiberianus were exiled to "insula Sylina, quæ ultra Britannias est." So wrote Sulpicius Severus, reporting the matter a few years later. The Bishops are believed to have founded the religious house on the island of Tresco which was developed into an Abbey a thousand years ago by Benedictine monks. This was some time after the Norsemen had ceased to use Scilly as a base for raiding Southern England.

Old John Leland, librarian to Henry VIII, wrote of Scilly, "Few men be glad to inabit these islettes, for al the plenty, for robbers by the sea that take their catail by force. The robbers be Frenchmen and Spaniardes . . . the owners of Scylley have scant 40 marks by yere of rentes and commodities of it."

With the dissolution of the monasteries in 1539 the "poore celle of Monkes" disappeared and the island passed to the Crown. For some years various piratical expeditions from France landed there, and in 1650 the Dutch admiral Van Tromp arrived with twelve men-of-war and prepared to raise his flag. He was resisted by the loyal governor, Sir John Granville. Complaints of these buccaneering sorties having been laid before Parliament, Admiral Blake was sent with a fleet to reduce and garrison the islands, a task not accomplished without bloodshed. A circular fort was built on Tresco; it is still called Oliver Cromwell's Castle.

From that time a perpetual peace has dwelt in these lovely islands. The alarms of the succeeding wars scarcely touched Scilly, although from time to time the garrison of St. Mary's and its guns were strengthened, as during the Spanish war, and the two world wars. At one time the garrison consisted of five invalided soldiers who manned some guns from a wreck salvaged after lying under the sea for over fifty years! It is said that modern guns cannot be fired safely without bringing down the walls of the storm-beaten dwellings of Scilly.

It was at the beginning of the present century that flowers began to be grown on a scale that brought the present prosperity to the islands. Before that the islanders lived by fishing and farming. Leland says "The ground . . berith exceeding corn, insomuch that if a man do but cast corn where hogges have rotid, it wyl cum up." And by smuggling, ship-building, and

Scale of Miles
0   100

Foula   SHETLANDS   LERWICK
ORKNEYS
Sumburgh Head
Fair Isle
N. Ronaldshay

Sula Sgeir   N. Ronay

Flannan Isles
Lewis
OUTER HEBRIDES
St. Kilda
Heiskier
Monach Is.
Harris
Uist
Skye   Rona
Barra   Canna   Raasay
Rum   Scalpay
Muck   Eigg
Coll
Tiree
Mull
Iona   OBAN
Scarba   Lunga
Colonsay
Jura   Bute
Islay   Cumbraes
Arran

SCOTLAND

The Bass Rock
Holy Island
Farne Islands

Tory Is.
Rathlin
Ailsa Craig
Aran

Isle of Man
Calf

Clare Is.
Inishturk
Inishbofin
Lambay
Skerries
Anglesey

IRELAND

Aran Islands

Bardsey

WALES

ENGLAND

Scolt Head

Great Blasket
Saltee
Dursey Is.
Clear Is.
Ramsey
Skomer
Skokholm
Caldey
Flatholm
Steepholm
Lundy
BIDEFORD BAY

Mersea
Canvey
Sheppey
Thanet

PENZANCE
Isles of Scilly

Isle of Wight

Alderney
Guernsey   Sark
Jersey

MAP OF THE BRITISH ISLES SHOWING THE CHIEF PLACES MENTIONED IN THE TEXT

ST. MARY, SCILLY ISLES
Water colour by J. C. Schetky

the burning of seaweed: activities which were of no great profit owing to
the distance from mainland markets. Often distress and want came to the
islands. An order had to be made prohibiting the export of corn, for the
islanders in dire straits for money frequently sold their corn to passing
ships, with resultant famine.

The collection and burning of seaweed to produce the alkali kelp was
an arduous performance which lasted as long as the ore-weed or laminaria
grew during the summer. Men, women and children worked at the cutting
and drying from dawn to dusk. The weed was thoroughly dried on the
beach before being burned in stone-lined pits in the sand. Each night a few
faggots of furze started the fire. Each kiln consumed a great quantity of the
weed in a slow fire lasting about five hours. Then the mass of weed would
suddenly liquefy, whereupon a dozen men would turn it over quickly with
long-handled iron forks, the sweat pouring from them. A. Quiller-Couch
describes how, at this exciting moment, the young women and girls would
dance in a chain around the men until they had finished working the
molten mass.

The kelp fires burned all over the islands, making the Scillonian
night seem to be a ring of bright jewels under the summer moon. But
the toil and sweat brought little more than a few pounds to each family, less
than was necessary to keep them over the winter.

ST. MICHAEL'S MOUNT
Engraving, 1804

Scilly was always noted for the quantity and size of her wild flowers, including the half-wild narcissus known as the Scilly White. But their possibilities for prosperity were scarcely suspected until in 1883 the governor, Mr. T. A. Dorrien-Smith, visited the bulb farms of Flanders, and foresaw that the Scilly climate would produce the newest varieties of daffodils, narcissi, wallflowers and lilies earlier than any other flower-growing district in range of the London market. It was from the considerable nucleus of new varieties which he imported and planted experimentally on Tresco that the islanders obtained most of the new stocks on which their present prolific output is based. To-day every cottager grows a quota of spring flowers. In March and April the gardens and little fields are filled with yellows and whites between the shelter hedges of escallonia and veronica. Something like two hundred tons of flowers are exported each week in the height of the season.

In addition to early flowers, early potatoes are marketed in May. There is also an all-the-year-round demand for holiday accommodation, with its attendant stimulus to the sale of dairy produce. So that between flowers, potatoes, visitors, dairy-farming, boating and fishing, the Scillonian is one of the most prosperous of the small islanders of Britain.

St. Mary's is the principal island, that is, the central one where the thrice-weekly steamer disgorges the tourists, empty flower-crates, mail and imports of corn and meat and groceries, and embarks the island produce and a stream of bronzed holiday-makers. To-day, if you wish, you can fly from Cornwall to St. Mary's. Hugh Town with its pier is the civic and shopping centre. Upon this pier converge the boats, including the official mail-boat, from the smaller islands of Tresco, famous for its semi-tropical gardens which surround the home of the governor and the ruins of the Abbey; Bryher with its five hills and its charming little town of about eighty inhabitants; St. Martins, where half the land slopes to the south and is warm and very early for flowers, and where the men are tall and fair and given to fishing; and St. Agnes, the smallest, the island of shipwrecks and sea-birds.

Save for some small grassy rocks such as St. Michael's Mount near Penzance, and some islets close along the Cornish shore, there are no islands worthy of the name until we reach the granite mass of Lundy, lying north and by west of Bideford Bay in Devon. A plane from Barnstaple is the quickest and generally the most pleasant method of crossing the Great White Horse Race where the Severn tides rip past the high plateau of Lundy.

This wild tide roost has helped to make Lundy semi-inaccessible by small boats. In contrast with the low and fertile Scillies, this elevated cliff-bound island has been almost uninhabited for nearly a century. At present its resident population comprises six keepers in charge of the North and South Lighthouses, and about a dozen others dependent on the establishment of hotel-cum-farm-cum-residence of the proprietor. With a plane service visitors now come for a few hours or days to see the sea-birds, the half-wild ponies, goats and several kinds of deer of this wild-life sanctuary. There are pheasants and partridges, and even squirrels and peacocks, and other representatives of European fauna have been more or less successfully acclimatised.

The cottages of the quarrymen, fishermen and smugglers who once inhabited the island lie in ruins about the settlement in the south-east corner of Lundy, where the owner's tree-embowered villa and a small church and the farm are the principal features. There is plenty of life on Lundy; you may study within its three-mile length (it is nowhere as much as a mile wide) almost a confusion of wild and semi-wild life, from the herds and flocks roaming the grassy plateau to the puffins, guillemots, razorbills, cormorants and gulls which nest in the steep sides of the 400-foot high cliffs. But of a self-contained and independent community, living from soil and sea as in Scilly, there is little sign. The island has an undistinguished history. It was the refuge and base of Norsemen who called it *Lunde-ey*, that is, the Island of Puffins. The Sallee Rovers visited it, and other pirates and the riff-raff of the Bristol Channel. Rats also arrived, and these have helped to reduce the numbers of the puffins. A small colony of gannets, nesting on a pinnacle in the north-east of the island, has abandoned this, then the only nesting-site in England, since about 1900.

Next and last island in our coastal tour of England is Steepholm, lying in the brown water at the mouth of the Severn, and claimed as part of Somerset, a high mass of rock containing little but an obsolete fort with sea-birds and sheld-ducks in the slopes below. It is now leased to a bird-lover who has declared it a sanctuary. Steepholm is widely known to botanists as the only home in Britain of the wild peony, *Paeonia officinalis*, native of the hills of southern Europe. Its lovely dark red flowers are, to quote Bentham and Hooker, "naturalised in the rocky clefts of the Steep Holme Island."

The Channel Islands, although owing allegiance to our King, are not, strictly speaking, islands round Britain. But they are so much a part of the British Nation both in war and peace that they deserve brief mention here. Nearest to England (as it is also nearest to France—at the Cherbourg peninsula) is Alderney, a long narrow rocky island with a sturdy breed of men who are small farmers, quarrymen and fishermen. In 1940 they were faced with the choice between immediate evacuation or remaining and coming under German domination. They did not hesitate. They removed the gates to allow their famous Alderney cattle to wander freely in search of food and water, and hurried to the boat waiting to take them to Britain, every man, woman and child. The other islands of Jersey, Guernsey and Sark, with their larger population, could not be more than partially evacuated in time. Jersey and Guernsey have their special breeds of cattle, developed as a result of centuries of breeding to suit local conditions. The islanders, who speak a French patois, have their own government, and live principally by trade with Britain, to which they export a large tonnage of early potatoes and tomatoes. Visitors also bring in a considerable revenue. Taxes are very low. Victor Hugo delighted to live in the mild frost-free climate of these productive islands, and it was here that he drew inspiration for his great novel *Toilers of the Sea*.

ST. CATHERINE'S BAY, ST. MARTIN'S, JERSEY
Coloured lithograph by P. J. Ouless, 1842

BLACK MARBLE QUARRY NEAR RED WHARF BAY, ANGLESEY
Drawn and engraved by William Daniell, 1813

ISLANDS ROUND WALES

THE little island of Flatholm is claimed as part of Glamorganshire. It is small, low, and has good pasture for a few cows. Until recently it boasted the only public house in the Bristol Channel, used, it is said, as a clearing house for up-channel smugglers and rum-runners—since there were no other inhabitants save the innkeeper. To-day there is little to see except the lighthouse and the isolation hospital (invariably empty) maintained by the Cardiff City corporation.

Caldey is the first worthy island of Wales. It lies to the south of Tenby, from which it is separated by a narrow strait affording good anchorage to coasting vessels which used to collect the limestone hewn from its north-facing cliffs. This rock is full of caves from which neolithic human and animal remains have been recovered. There are written records (the lives of St. Samson and St. Paul de Leon especially) showing that a monastery existed in the sixth century. The island was then called Pyr, the first abbot being Piro, and he was drowned, as more than one monk has since been, in crossing the tide-races.

Norsemen knew and named Caldey (the Island of the Spring). Illtyd, Dubricius, David and Gildas were saints who worked in the Celtic monastery before the Norman conquest. In the reign of Henry I it was conveyed to the great Benedictine house of St. Dogmaels, of which it remained a cell until the dissolution of the monasteries. It was thereafter in private hands until 1907, when a community of Anglican Benedictines bought the island and "came home." That is to say, they set about building the present magnificent red-roofed white-stuccoed abbey which gives the island a Mediterranean air. The Benedictines were generous in their expenditure and planning. They set up lathes and work-benches, and, inspired by their leader, the Abbot Aelred, endeavoured to make the island a self-supporting entity by exploiting its possibilities for local industries : pottery, leather goods, agricultural produce, a poultry farm, even the tourist trade was catered for by the running of a guest house, the building and letting of private houses, a shop, and a daily steamer. Aelred finally decided to join the Roman communion, and this defection, together with the advent of the first world war, brought the community deeper than ever into financial troubles. The appeal for funds was not successful; the community was compelled to sell out and migrate to join a mainland community at Prinknash in Gloucestershire.

A sterner community of monks—Cistercians of the Strict Observance from the Trappist foundation of Chimay in Belgium—bought Caldey. Their pursuit is strictly religious and agricultural, their life abstemious. They have succeeded well in spite of loss of part of the monastery by fire, and the destruction of the mother house by the German military machine in the second world war.

Caldey has many pleasant private houses upon it, each with its large flower and fruit gardens, most of them built in the "Benedictine period." These are occupied chiefly by retired persons who enjoy the warm frost-free climate, the flowers, fuchsia, conifers and trees and sand of Priory Bay and the village. There are no rates or taxes. The maintenance of the island's electricity, inter-house telephone service, bakery and ferry—relics of Benedictine enterprise—is still the task of the Trappists, whose main service, however, is one of prayer. Visitors are not encouraged, and the island is closed on Sundays. To pray and to work in peace; if you wish to do only these things, you will be welcome, for no genuine wayfarer in search of God may be refused sanctuary.

The day for the Cistercian monk begins with matins and lauds at 2 a.m. The lay brothers, who wear long beards and brown habit, go out to milk the cows at 4 a.m., while the choir religious, wearing the white habit, remain at devotion. The day's work, in which all brothers share, is given out at 5.30 a.m., and begins after pittance (breakfast) and high mass are completed at 8.45 a.m. Dinner at 11.30 and work again from 1 to 5 p.m. when vespers begin. Collation (supper) at 5.30, followed by compline, and bed at 7 p.m., or 8 if the harvest is in full swing. The diet consists of soup, bread, fruit, milk, butter and coffee.

The Caldey farm, 600 acres, is run on a scientific routine of balanced cropping and stock-raising so as to maintain its fertility and its exports of cattle, sheep, pigs, wheat, oats, barley, vegetables and butter, by which the community pays its way. The land is fertile, part overlying limestone and part red sandstone, and the crops mature about one month earlier than those of the rest of South Wales.

In the south-east of Caldey is a wood of pines, poplars and rhododendrons; here the monks have a shrine, and here bullfinches and goldfinches and many tree-loving birds make their sanctuary. The wild cliffs of the south side are the haunt of sea-birds.

To the west of Caldey and accessible at low water by a climb over boulders and by skirting shrimping pools, is St. Margaret's Isle, its limestone much quarried in the past and carved by man and sea into several steep holms. Cormorants occupy some of these. One holm is pinnacled with old buildings of an ecclesiastical character, their lay-out suggesting a chapel, refectory and dormitory. Wild flowers and small singing birds upon its walls and the wind in rank weeds below them cannot quite conceal the flavour of departed greatness. Recently this ancient roofless cell, whose history has only been guessed at, was occupied by a modern recluse. Charlie was the son of a Tenby boatman. He grew up to be what was locally termed a "main queer crut," which, roughly translated, means that as a man he was still a boy with a boy's ambitions. He had a passion for, and claimed St. Margaret's Isle as his own. Charlie is since dead but when I last visited the islet I found surviving him several rough notice-boards painted in a boyish hand "Charlie's Island—Sea Birds' Sanctuary—Private." Charlie is remembered kindly now, and in Tenby they smile proudly when they tell how he used to daub warning notices along the cliff-face, and how he used to threaten anyone who tried to land while he was in residence during the sea-bird season. He sailed a small boat between his hut on the mainland and the island, and would remain on St. Margaret's as long as his food lasted.

Off the extreme west of Pembrokeshire lie the rugged group of small islands with Norse names, whose high cliffs are filled from April to August with nesting sea-birds. Farthest west is Grassholm, the "green islet," about twenty-two acres, waterless and remarkable as the home of some 14,000 gannets. Grassholm's history has little to do with man and all to do with the weather and the sea-birds—an ecological picture. Its volcanic basalt rose from the sea—it has a raised beach to prove this—naked until spore and seed took root. Centuries later, when the deposit of dead vegetation, built up by perennial grasses living on moisture and the dead roots of their ancestors, was three feet thick, the island was invaded by thousands of burrowing puffins. These turned the haystack crown of Grassholm into a metropolis of underground burrows. The island became a vast puffin slum by the middle of the last century. Then the flimsy ceilings and roofs and walls collapsed under the strain of summer excavation and winter storms. The puffins gradually deserted the island, moving eastwards to the islands

GANNET
Engraving from T. Pennant's *A Tour in Scotland*, 1799

of Skomer and Skokholm. Meanwhile gannets had colonised the high west cliffs, and after a period of persecution by fishermen, they have gradually increased under the active wardenship of the Pembrokeshire Bird Protection Society, until to-day there are something like 7,000 pairs nesting. As each pair has its nesting pedestal within approximately one square yard of territory, the 7,000 nests about cover two acres.

The plumage of the adult gannet is a very hard white, the head tinged with gold, the bill is plumbeous, the eye cold and pale, the wing-tips jet black, while the black webbed feet have longitudinal blue-green stripes or "clocks" running down from the thigh to the tips of the toes. Gazed upon from the convenient ridge which crowns Grassholm, with the sun and the

23

bright blue of the sea to help, the whole scene of the gannetry is as dazzling and lovely as it is unique.

Skokholm, nearest island to the mouth of Milford Haven, is lower; and its red sandstone gives it a warmer appearance, in contrast with the grey basalt of its larger and higher sister island of Skomer to the north. Both are noted bird sanctuaries. Both once held prosperous farms, but to-day farmers and their labourers will not face the isolation, and until there are freight-carrying planes which can land and take off without runways, transport difficulties make island farming an uneconomical business. At present agricultural goods have to be handled five times: from lorry to mainland embarking stage, from stage to boat, from boat to island beach, from beach to cart, and from cart to farm; or vice versa.

The islands of Skomer and Skokholm remain attractively wild, their fields overrun with sea-birds and wild flowers, their swards grazed by innumerable rabbits, with heather, bracken and thrift advancing from the boundaries to which they were driven in the few centuries when man laboured to fence and farm the islands.

Skomer has a great wedge driven into her high south cliffs. The sea enters this Wick, and throws much driftwood upon an inaccessible beach where seals sleep and breed. Above are cliffs 250 feet high with wide ledges upon which a horse and cart might be driven; these are covered with thousands of murmuring sea-birds and gulls. Nowhere south of the great loomeries of the Scottish islands can such a wealth and variety of sea-bird life be studied. Puffins fill the topmost earthy layers where the sea-pinks and white campion blow in the moist west wind. In the fissures of basalt are peregrine falcons, buzzards, ravens, kestrels, choughs and jackdaws. Then come the ledges packed with the "eligugs" as the South Pembroke-shire fishermen call the guillemots, and in the debris and under boulders are the less communal razorbills. Close to the water's edge, where the cliff wall is smoother, the kittiwake has its nest on every slight foothold.

Skokholm has the distinction of being the first site in the British Isles where a bird observatory and bird-marking station has been established, on the lines of the famous ornithological observatory at Heligoland. Here, until war interrupted the work, up to 6,000 birds were ringed annually, a proportion of these being adult migrants trapped in special cages and marked with aluminium leg-rings and released. The recovery elsewhere of an average of under 3 per cent. of these travellers has led to a clearer knowledge of their migrations, both local and continental. Extensive ringing of sea-birds proved that the Manx shearwater can leave the nest at Skokholm, wander six hundred miles south to feed on the sardines on the North Spanish coast, and return a few days later to give its sitting mate a spell off the egg, or to give the young chick a good feed once in two or three days. Ringing of gannets at Grassholm by the Skokholm Bird Observatory led to the discovery that the young birds of the year fly farthest south, reaching

By courtesy of the Walker Galleries, London

HOLY ISLAND

Water colour by John Varley, 1778-1842

GENERAL VIEW OF GUERNSEY FROM PORT GEORGE

Water colour by R. P. Leitch, c. 1850

By gracious permission of H.M. The King

the Capricorn coast off Mauretania during winter. But the adult gannets, as they get older, seem to remain closer to the gannetry throughout the year.

North of Skomer, across the graceful arc of St. Brides Bay, is Ramsey, which in 1326 paid tithes to the Bishop of St. David's at the rate of twopence per head for the 10 horses, 100 cattle, and 300 sheep grazed there. As well as twopence per acre for the "two carucates of land containing 100 acres."

A good farm still survives on Ramsey's 600 acres ; thanks to the enterprise of the tenant in co-operation with the owner, the land and buildings are coming back into good heart again.

All the Pembrokeshire islands, including the small islet of forty acres known as Cardigan Island, off the mouth of the river Teify, are held as nature reserves by agreement with tenant or owner under the aegis of the Pembrokeshire Bird Protection Society.

The next small Welsh Island is Bardsey, off the extremity of Carnarvonshire. It is reputed to be the resting-place of 20,000 saints, martyrs and holy men, whose innumerable grave-stones are said to crop up in the fields and roads everywhere—the prosaic geologist may tell you this is due to the perpendicular position of underlying slate strata. In A.D. 420 Einion Frenhin founded a religious house—its few remaining stones can still be seen. To live and die and be buried on Bardsey ensured, it is said, immortality. But more prosaic reasons have induced the colonisation of the island by Welsh peasants of the hardy Carnarvonshire breed. The low-lying half of Bardsey is very fertile, there is good rough grazing on the mountainous eastern half, the buildings are excellent; having been reconstructed seventy years ago with money obtained from the sale of the shipping dues and lighthouse site to Trinity House. The farmhouses are built in pairs, semi-detached. Each farmer has his own farm offices sufficient to house three cows, a horse, and pigs. He shares the yard and a cart with his neighbour. He works an average of twenty-five acres, plus hill grazing rights. Co-operation on the island extends to the sharing of the expense and working of the mail-boat. Because it is essentially practical and economic this co-operation in daily work is worth all the loose theorising and talk about community values indulged in by idealists who sip their morning coffee in ultra-fashionable urban cafés. Those who dream of island community life—and there are many seeking this form of millennium—would do well to spend a year on Bardsey, and see whether they are really prepared to endure the isolation and exposure and hard work which is the price the islanders must pay for a healthy life, a low rent, fairly comfortable houses, and a chance to save money. The three dozen inhabitants of Bardsey, like the people of Scilly, survive by successful small farming, with fishing and visitors as profitable side-lines which enable the islanders to buy such luxuries as radio sets, books and gramophones. Exports are black cattle,

ROPE BRIDGE NEAR THE LIGHTHOUSE, HOLY HEAD
Drawn and engraved by William Daniell, 1813

sheep, pigs, poultry, eggs, rabbits, butter and fish. Furze is cut green at two years' growth and chaffed with hay and straw to feed cattle and horses. The people of Bardsey at present are a comparatively young colonisation, individually young too, and much given to hospitality, intelligent conversation, and singing and competing at the main cultural event of the Welsh year, the eisteddfod.

Anglesey, Wales' largest island, connected to Carnarvonshire by a famous suspension bridge, is a land of soft undulations and low-lying pastures filled with the hardy rich-milking black cattle of Wales. Its moors and lakes and marshes abound with wild fowl. Celtic culture from the time of the Druids to the foundation of the Celtic church has many monuments and remains up and down the two hundred square miles of the island's surface. The student of pre-history will find a rich field for research in the numberless ancient stones scattered over each parish or in few cases preserved in the "llan" or church. The same can be said of the long straggling and indented Holyhead Island, connected by bridges and sands to the north-west side of Anglesey. While off Carmel Head in the extreme north-west are the Skerries, a group of rocks given over to a lighthouse and colonies of sea-swallows. Puffin Island in the east and Llanddwyn Island in the south-west, also sea-bird sanctuaries, are other satellite islets of Anglesey.

26

PUFFIN ISLAND, ANGLESEY
Drawn and engraved by William Daniell, 1813

THE ISLE OF MAN

ALTHOUGH the Isle of Man is neither English nor Scotch, it has associations with both countries. It has its own government, the House of Keys, which adopts—with modifications to suit local conditions—most of the Acts passed by the House of Commons. But its lighthouses are manned by keepers in the service of the (Scottish) Commissioners of Northern Lights. And the lighthouse on Douglas Head is a familiar and welcome sight to the thousands of visitors to this, Britain's most popular if most isolated island holiday resort, when it is first sighted towards the end of the seventy-mile sea passage between Liverpool and Douglas. The mill and factory hands of Lancashire and the North Midlands find in Man's rugged coast and beautiful glens (Sulby, Laxey, Dhoon and Helen are best known) and seaside entertainment fare everything to satisfy the desire for the perfect short holiday, while the four-hour run over an often rough sea in the steamer is a hazard which adds spice to the journey and shakes up the jaded system. The new airfields which have been built in Man since the outbreak of war have made the transport by air liners of a large proportion of the holiday makers of the future a probability. But it is only the resident and the visitor with ample time who learns to love the wilder parts of this beautiful island, who can tramp over the moors of Snaefell and the Barrules, and explore the wild flats of the Ayre in the north part of Man, and become acquainted with the political system of a government which is modelled on the ancient Viking Tingvald.

Man's only island, the Calf, has a lighthouse, and it once held a thriving farm. The usual tale of isolation and loneliness and agricultural depression holds good here. The farm declined, rabbits and sea-birds took possession. Finally the danger of exploitation by private enterprise was removed when the National Trust acquired the Calf and placed a resident watcher there. The island is situated in the stream of Irish Sea migration, and has fine colonies of sea-birds. It should become a future migratory and sea-bird study station.

THE CATHEDRAL, ISLE OF MAN
Seventeenth century engraving

LOCH SCAVIG, ISLE OF SKYE
Drawn and engraved by William Daniell, 1813

ISLANDS ROUND SCOTLAND

"O THESE endless little isles" wrote Muir, his heart caught with his deep pleasure as he thought of the vast archipelago of the Hebrides. And well might the perplexed historiographer echo him. But I attempt no catalogue. That would be impossible within the confines of this book. I merely give samples, for I am as unwearied as was Muir with the prospect of never coming to an end of exploring and enjoying the endless little isles of Scotland. Much has been written about them, but there remains much more to be seen and told and collected. The Kennedy Frasers have achieved much in their recent collection of Hebridean music. And Seton Gordon, living in the far north of the great island of Skye, has with camera and pen sketched a portion of the beauty of these islands, their story and their natural history, in his books written from Duntuilm. Fraser Darling is engaged with others in an attempt to re-organise the lives of the crofters of the Hebrides so as to meet the post-war difficulties. It is certain that the small farmer of the north-west cannot survive on the fruits of his few peaty and stony acres. But the old customs still cling to

CIRCLE OF STONES AT TURMORE, ISLE OF ARRAN
Water colour by W. A. Nesfield, 1793-1881

the islands in spite of the economic insecurity which is depopulating them. It is also interesting to note the persistence of the Catholic faith, untouched by the Reformation, on Barra and other islands.

Take first the islands of the Clyde, of which the principal ones are Arran, Bute and the Cumbraes. Hundreds of people working in Glasgow offices find the amenities of island life in Bute and the Cumbraes outweigh its disadvantages; they travel to work by steamer every morning. Arran with its moors and lakes and mountains provides the Highland scene in miniature.

There are many small islands in the Clyde: of which the strangest must be the rock of Ailsa Craig. Sir William Brereton wrote in July 1635—the words in brackets are mine—"Upon the way hence (from Glasgow) we discovered many islands, and amongst the rest one more remarkable isle, hence shows itself at forty mile distant; this is placed about sixteen (actually nine) miles from the shore. It is a mighty high rock, seeming very steep and high (it is 1,113 feet high), round at the top; the name of it is Ellsey; not inhabited, but with abundance of fowl and two earies of Goose-hawks, this year stolen by Highlanders. This rock was in our view three days whilst we travelled betwixt sixty and seventy mile, and when you are at a great distance, it presents itself in shape like a sugar-loaf, and when you approach nearer it seems lower and flatter at the top, but it is a much-to-be-admired piece of the Lord's workmanship. In this isle breed abundance of Solemne Geese (gannets) which are longer-necked and bodied than ours, and so extreme fat are the young that when they eat them, they are placed in the middle of the room, so as all may have access about it; their arms stripped up and linen cloaths placed before their cloaths, to secure them from being defiled from the fat thereof, which doth besprinkle and besmear all that come near unto it."

Gannets were also taken for food from the Bass Rock on the other side of Scotland, in the Firth of Forth, the Bass being about one third the size of Ailsa. Quite a voluminous literature exists, proving that the "Soland-geese" were a source of profit to the owner of the Rock. The 120 soldiers who garrisoned the "Castle of Bass" in 1548 were said to "live for the most part on nothing else than the fish daily carried thither by these birds." Not an impossible story; if you walk about among nesting gannets you can easily collect basket-loads of almost fresh fish disgorged by the frightened birds who in this way lighten themselves before flying off. The eggs and young birds also provided food, and the large hummock nests of seaweed

THE BASS ROCK
Drawing by J. M. W. Turner engraved by W. Millar

31

and flotsam made good fuel when dried. The fat of the gannet was used as a salve, sovereign against many human ills, and useful for greasing cart-wheels.

As late as 1876 the Bass gannets were sold for food, many going to Sheffield, and, in order to keep them sweet, they were first plucked, wrapped in rhubarb leaves, and partly cooked, in large ovens, four at a time. The eggs fetched six shillings a dozen. The rent of the Bass in 1535 was four hundred gold pieces, such was the value of the birds then. In 1841 it had dropped to £30.

The greatest gannet colony in the world is that of St. Kilda, estimated in 1939 to contain nearly 17,000 pairs of nesting gannets on three stacks called Lee, An Arnim, and Boreray. For the early information on St. Kilda we owe much to a little book of 158 pages entitled "A Late Voyage to St. Kilda, the Remotest of all the Hebrides or Western Isles of Scotland, A History of the Island, Natural, Moral, and Topographical. Wherein is an Account of their Customs, Religion, Fish, Fowl, etc. As also a Relation of a late Impostor, pretended to be sent by St. John Baptist, by M. Martin, Gent, 1698."

Martin had a perilous voyage there, and nearly missed the Isles. By watching the flights of gannets he steered safely to the shelter of Boreray, which at that time fed 400 sheep and had 40 "stone Pyramids for drying and preserving their Fowls, as well as lodging the Inhabitants that attend the Seasons of the Solan Geese." He visited An Arnim and returned with 800 dried gannets from the previous year, which were shared out among the St. Kildans, each bird having been marked on the foot by its owner.

Martin found 180 people living on Hirta, the main island of the group. They were in a flourishing condition, except for two families with a touch of leprosy due to eating tainted flesh. Martin estimated that the islanders consume yearly 22,600 gannets, which would be about as much as 17,000 pairs could raise to maturity in two years. His figures are none too reliable, however. Perhaps he included fulmar petrels in this figure—for centuries this bird has been used in great quantity by the people of St. Kilda, originally its sole nesting site in Britain. Martin says the St. Kildans assigned him and his crew a maintenance of the Hirtan diet, which consisted of fish, mutton, milk, sea-birds and their eggs, their generosity being such that eighteen guillemots' eggs were allowed per diem per man. Martin's men developed a feverish condition from eating so much protein.

At that time a year or two might pass without a boat reaching this lonely community. A healthy primitive tradition was observed under a factor-minister, with the "Christ Church" as the centre. As coin of the realm had almost no purchasing power on St. Kilda, rent was paid with puffins and feathers. The men made ropes out of horse-hair. They used gannet oil for their lamps and also (1875) exported 600 gallons of gannet and fulmar oil yearly. They obtained their fishing-hooks from the stomachs

ST. HELIER, JERSEY
Water colour by J. Young

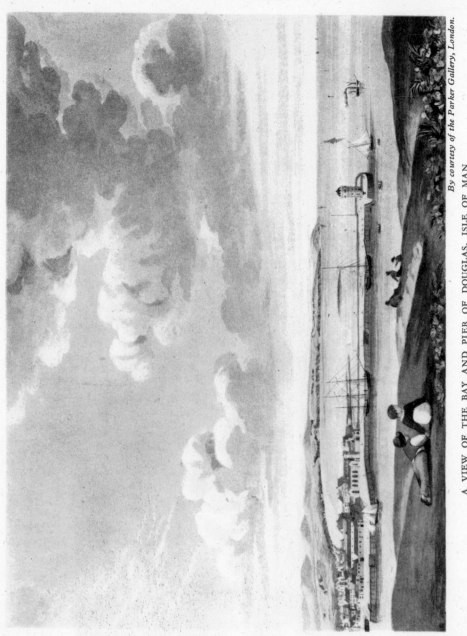

A VIEW OF THE BAY AND PIER OF DOUGLAS, ISLE OF MAN

Coloured engraving by J. Burman

of gannets which had evidently devoured fish escaped from lines laid by fishermen in Scottish and even English waters.

With the advent of the yearly and later the monthly summer steamer, trouble and dissatisfaction came to Hirta's street of small thatched homes. The itinerant merchants sold their rubbishy trinkets and tinned food for high prices to the islanders, giving them a whiff of the excitements of the world beyond the sea-birds' cries, and incidentally leaving them enough streptococci germs to send several islanders to the grave with "steamer cold" as the influenza was ever after called on Hirta. The high prices realised for the island produce—chiefly feathers and oil—fell almost to nil, and the men began leaving the island at the beginning of the present century. To-day Hirta village is empty, sheep and wild birds run over the little fields where the bare-legged St. Kildan lassies once called their cows with a handful of dock leaves to lure them to the milking yard.

Even more lonely perhaps is North Ronay, which lies 45 miles N.W. of Cape Wrath, and about the same distance N.E. of the Butt of Lewis. Again we have to thank Martin Martin for our early knowledge. He obtained it from a minister of Barvas in Lewis, in whose parish Ronay lay. There were then (about 1700) five families who "have cows, sheep, barley, oats, and live a harmless life, being perfectly ignorant of most of the vices which abound in the world. They know nothing of money or gold, having no occasion for either; they covet no wealth, being fully satisfied with food and raiment; though at the same time they are very precise in the matter of property among themselves; for none of them will by any means allow his neighbour to fish within his property. They have an agreeable and hospitable temper for all strangers. They take their surname from the colour of the sky, rainbow, and clouds. Every tenant hath his dwelling house, a barn, a house for their cattle, and a porch on each side of the door to keep off rain, and snow. Their houses are built with stone and thatched with straw, which is kept down with ropes of the same, poised with stones. They wear the same habit with those in Lewis, and speak only Irish." One islander who wanted a wife, having got a shilling from a seaman who happened to land there, gave this shilling to the minister to purchase him a wife in Lewis, for he was told that this piece of money had an extraordinary value; the minister sent him a woman by the next (yearly) boat.

The whole ancient race of Ronans died out when a swarm of rats landed and ate up their corn, and at the same time some seamen robbed them of their bull. The steward of St. Kilda, happening to be storm-driven there, found the last inhabitant, a woman, dead with a child at her breast.

Ronay was recolonised. We learn that a cottar was bound to the island for eight years, and was not allowed a boat in case he was tempted to sail for Ness and get drowned. "There is a chapel in the midst of the isle, where they meet twice or thrice a day. One of the families is hereditary beddal, and . . . stands at the altar and prayeth, the rest kneels upon their knees and join with him. Their religion is the Romish religion . . . they are so well satisfied with their condition that they exceedingly bewail the condition of those, as supernumery, they must send out of the island.''

It is now a hundred years since Ronay has been occupied by other than the sheep brought from Ness and an occasional student of birds and seals. In 1885 two men of Ness, wishing to atone for an unworthy opposition to their minister, resolved to go into exile on Ronay. They sailed on the morning of 20th May 1884, and landed the same night. Twice before winter friends went out to persuade them to return to their families, only to find the men apparently happy in sheep-tending, fishing and sealing, and reading the Gaelic scriptures. They kept tally of the days by notching a piece of driftwood, making a deeper notch for Sundays, and a cut from side to side for the end of the month. The marking began on 21st of June 1884 and ceased on 17th February 1885. The bodies of the two men were found on 22nd April 1885, in the half-underground houses of Ronay; the survivor had placed his tartan plaid with loving care over his comrade's body. There was ample store of food.

In 1936 two young naturalists, J. A. Ainslie and R. Atkinson, camped by the ruined chapel which they found occupied by sea-birds, one of which, the rare Leach's fork-tailed petrel, they studied intensively. At the present day the island is associated with the work of Fraser Darling on the Atlantic seals which breed there. All will agree with his dictum that North Ronay must be made a perpetual nature reserve.

Before leaving the outermost fringe of the Outer Hebrides, we should explore another haunt of the fork-tailed petrel—the Flannan Isles or Seven Hunters, lying west of Lewis. The greatest, Eilean Mor, is 288 feet high, covers 39 acres, grazes 30 sheep, and holds the ruin of St. Flannan's chapel and a lighthouse. The men of Lewis observe certain superstitions when they land on the Seven Hunters to collect sheep and sea-birds. Martin says the first is ''not to ease nature in that place where the boat lies . . . a crime of the highest. . . they have a great regard to that very piece of rock upon which they first set their feet, after escaping the danger of the ocean.'' Certain places and things must not be mentioned by their usual names. There is, or was, a whole catalogue of rites, presumably induced by the fears and hazards which attended their visit to these lonely islands. The Flannans, lovely though they look to the visitor who sees them by the light of the summer sea, have a sinister reputation, which has been enhanced by the following tragedy. Not long after the lighthouse was erected on Eilean Mor, a passing ship reported that the light was not exhibited. Some days later the relief boat made its rounds, but no one met it at the landing-steps. A long search failed to discover the three keepers. The mystery of their disappearance has not yet been solved. Wilfrid Gibson has since put in verse the feeling of despair which seems to haunt the landing-place:

INTERIOR OF A FOULA COTTAGE
Woodcut, 1878

"We landed; and made fast the boat,
And climbed the track in single file,
Each wishing he were safe afloat,
On any sea, however far,
So be it far from Flannan Isle."

Even now I have not described the remaining outermost isles of the Hebrides: Sule Sgeir, near Ronay, containing many gannets and petrels; Heiskier with its great seal colony, and the Monach Isles (where two lighthouse-keepers lost their lives in trying to return to the lighthouse) lying to the west of Uist. All were once visited and exploited by the men of the Long Island (Outer Hebrides), but now given over to the ways of waves and wind and wild nature. The same tale runs through all the remote islands of the Hebrides. Even the smallest skerry, such as might graze a canoeload of sheep, has some sign of human work and love—a farmhouse, a stone shelter, a sheep park, a boundary, often the chapel or cell of some little-known saint. But economic depression, due to bad government by leaders and politicians who, by manipulating home and overseas trade, sought to concentrate wealth into the hands of the literate few, has steadily depleted the population of the Highlands and Islands, and the first to go has been the sturdy race of small islanders. Only in a very few of the little islands of the Hebrides does a remnant survive to-day, and most of these are entirely dependent on the goodwill and financial assistance of the landlord. Such names as Raasay (where Bonnie Prince Charlie hid), Scalpay,

35

Eriskay, Vatersay, Mingulay, Berneray, the Summer Isles, South Rona, Ascrib and Soay of Skye, bring to mind the former glory of their fishermen-farmers, a scene of spiralling smoke and thatched homes, horses and kine, the bustle of women and children about the boats and the little fields of corn: the scene to-day is one of decayed cottages, derelict fields and havens and quays, and an old and pauperised and rapidly vanishing people.

Even in the few islands where there is an energetic resident proprietor, such as at Canna and Muck and Eigg, the population yearly declines. The lovely island of Rum with its five mountain peaks, each over 2,000 feet high, held 443 souls in 1795: to-day it has only a handful of servants attached to its owner's house, and the visitor is not welcome to wander with the deer through the deserted fields, or stub his toes on the moss and grass-hidden stones of cottages razed to the ground. The same tale is true of Scarba and other large islands of the Inner Hebrides which have been turned into private playgrounds and game preserves for the rich. The smaller, more exposed islands, such as the Ascribs, Lunga, the Holy Isles of the Sea, have become sheep-runs. Lunga, which lies north of Scarba and the whirl-pool of Corrievreckan, once held several families farming nine hundred acres. It has wood, water, good grass, peat, a warm aspect and a safe harbour. Two brothers graze sheep on Lunga and on the Black and the Holy Isles which lie south of the great island of Mull. They live on the slate-quarrying island of Luing, opposite Lunga, from which you take a short ferry to Seil Island, and Seil in turn is connected to Argyllshire and the Oban Road by a beautifully arched bridge, which is said locally to be the only bridge over the Atlantic. (This of course is not so; there is a bridge to Dana Island in the Sound of Jura. Achill in the west of Ireland and Anglesey and Holy-head Island in Wales have bridges over salt tidal water).

To reach Lunga and Scarba you have to cross Seil and Luing. This is often the best way to explore thoroughly the Hebrides, by using ferries and small boats from one island to another. You can always fall back on the little mail steamers which leave Oban and Mallaig and Tobermory, and which faithfully carry the tourists, cattle and sheep by which the islander lives. A favourite excursion by steamer is from Oban, via Iona and Staffa to Tobermory in Mull. Staffa with its columnar basalt caves is worth visiting—a day should be spent in a small boat exploring Staffa, and looking at the sea-birds and the colonies of seals on Treshnish. To the west lies the low fertile island of Tiree, with its fine airport promising the shape of the air travel in the freedom to come. I prefer to approach Iona by the long road which threads through the mountains and moors and by the woods and lochs of Mull to Fhionnphort, a village from which you look across the sound to Iona and its famous cathedral.

It was on the 12th of May A.D. 563, that the skin-covered curragh in which Columba, prince and monk, had sailed from Ireland, reached Iona. Columba desired to settle in some lonely spot from which his native land,

IONA CATHEDRAL
Engraving, 1838

even from the highest hill on the island, could not be seen. Here, safe in the heart of the Hebrides, while wars raged down the centuries, the cell of St. Columba was consecrated, and it has remained to this day—it is now the home of the Iona Community—a shrine of Christian teaching visited by kings and saints and the many whose faith has needed new inspiration.

Working round the north of Scotland, we come to the hundred isles of Shetland, with the fishing port of Lerwick as capital. The most westerly is Foula (Old Norse: *Fugley*, Bird-island). Agricola's Roman fleet, anchored in Orkney, saw on the horizon the sea-bird-whitened walls of Foula rising a thousand feet sheer from the sea to the north, and were certain they had seen Ultima Thule. Foula is fourteen miles west of Waas, the small Shetland port to which the mail boat manned by the islanders comes once a week. To the east of Foula lies the shallow cod-fishing bank "Shaalds of Foola," famed in Shetland song. There are about 100 people still on Foula; they live by fishing and crofting. The old trade in sea-birds, their eggs and feathers is dying out. Foula is one of the finest sea-bird sanctuaries in the world, and not to have seen the great cliffs of the Kaim, 1221 feet high and only eight degrees off perpendicular is not to have seen Shetland at all. To get the right perspective you need to cruise round Foula, standing some distance offshore. The whole coast is a series of sheer cliffs, stacks,

37

WRECK OF THE 'LESSING,' FAIR ISLE
Woodcut

and gios or gorges. Fulmar petrels, Manx shearwaters, great and arctic skuas, are notable among the milliards of nesting birds.

Fair Isle, "Britain's loneliest inhabited island," stands midway between the southern point of Shetland (28 miles distant), and the northern tip of Orkney (30 miles distant). It is claimed as part of Dunrossness, the most southern parish of Shetland; its principal features—the Ward Hill and the Sheep Craig — can be seen rising from the wild roost or tide-race from Sumburgh Head on a clear day. Its three square miles are bounded by high cliffs and great fissures or gios, and by caves and beaches where birds and seals abound. In May 1868 the population of 500 was doubled overnight by the wreck of the German barque *Lessing*, with 465 emigrants on board. In five weeks, while waiting for a relief ship, the foreigners devoured the whole of the food and fish, the cattle, sheep and pigs of the islanders. Communications are better for the 100 or less inhabitants to-day; they have their own powerful new decked motor boat which runs between the island and Sumburgh Head, and is subsidised by the G.P.O. Their living comes from cattle, sheep and fishing —principally for haddocks.

The Fair Isle man still ploughs the "inmark" (cultivated land) with oxen, borrowing a second ox from his neighbour. He plants chiefly "bere," a kind of barley used for making bread, and potatoes, with some roots and oats for the stock. This he does in March and April. In May the lambs come, and in this month the peat-cutting begins on the Ward Hill. Each family celebrates a peat-cutting day, inviting their neighbours to join in a picnic and arranging competitions for the men, who dig and throw the peats out, and for the women, who lay them out to dry. From June to September the chickens are all shut into houses to avoid damage to growing crops. In July the wool is "rooed" (pulled) off the native sheep, a small hardy breed, and the "plantycrubs" (small stone-walled enclosures) are set with home-saved cabbage seed. In these shelters the cabbages survive the winter-storms, and are planted out in the fields in the spring. The thin hay crop is gathered in July, the bere in August, the oats in September, the potatoes and roots in October. At all favourable times the men go in small boats to fish close off the east shore. Each cottage kitchen is by November filled with strings of drying haddocks, which, together with the peat-reek, give the Fair Isle homes a characteristic whiff.

These things occupy the life of the Fair Islander, and give him a deep love for his lonely home land. The women spin the native wool and knit jumpers and scarves and gloves with patterns carrying the world-famous X design. This is said to have been handed down from the Armada Spaniards who were wrecked when the flagship *El Gran Grifon* ran ashore in 1588. It is however more likely that the design is of Scandinavian origin, as well as the art of dyeing the hosiery with natural pigments. To-day the genuine Fair Isle jersey bears the special trade mark which reads "Fair Isle made in Fair Isle," to distinguish it from the equally well made jumper of the same patterns made on the mainland of Shetland and marked "Fair Isle made in Shetland."

With the improvement of aeroplane design to suit small landing grounds the day cannot be far off when a regular air service will connect Fair Isle with Shetland and Orkney. Steps are already being taken to set up on Fair Isle the third British Bird Observatory, part of a chain of such stations

DRONGS IN THE BAY OF ST. MAGNUS
Engraving, 1822

39

around the British Isles. Its isolation in the path of birds migrating from Scandinavia and Iceland makes it one of our most valuable sites for this purpose. It is renowned for the number of rare species visiting there in spring and autumn.

It was at Scatness near Sumburgh head that Betty Mouat, an invalid of sixty, lived. She had embarked in a sailing smack for Lerwick on January 30th, 1886. The skipper was accidentally knocked overboard soon after the smack sailed. The two men forming his crew went to his rescue in the ship's boat, and while they were doing so the sails of the smack came before the wind and she raced off into the North Sea. For eight days and nights the *Columbine* drifted, while the sick woman, unable to handle sheet or tiller, put her trust in prayer. The smack came to rest on a Norwegian island, moving unguided through rocky channels to a safe landing. Betty was hospitably received and cared for. On her return to Lerwick she was given a tremendous reception.

Out Skerries, nearest land to Norway, has a grim economy, since the three small islands, composing this most easterly of the Shetland group, are very stony and infertile. The eighty inhabitants are dependent on the sea; the men fish or go to sea in naval or merchant craft, the women look after the cows and sheep and poultry, and cultivate the "run-riggs," patches of soil won by hand from between the heaped rocks. Here bere and potatoes are grown, with seaweed for humus. There are no draught animals; the women carry the "ware" (seaweed) in "cassays" (straw panniers), dig by hand, and drag harrows in team together. They cut corn with a sickle, and hand-flail it. They are a simple happy lot, but few of the young people are willing to set up house there to-day. The modern houses are built simply enough of concrete, for which the islanders obtain sand and gravel and stones in plenty from the island itself.

In contrast with the ragged high barren and mist-swept rocks of Shetland the islands of the Orkneys are most of them smooth low fertile and sunny. The Shetlander is a fisherman with a croft, the Orcadian a farmer with a boat. Orcadian farms are three or four times as large as Shetland holdings. The land rises and falls with gentle swells, with wide horizons, and here and there broad lochs catching the reflection of sunlit clouds. Most of the islands have good airfields. There is a pleasing neatness about the grey stone-built houses and the solid farm buildings, with their round corn ricks thatched with plaited straw. The fields grow prosperous crops, each island exporting a share of the cattle, sheep, grain and eggs for which Orkney is noted. The islanders farm on modern lines, paying attention to high-yielding grass leys of short duration as part of their arable system. The horses are large and strong, and totally unlike the diminutive Shetland ponies. Fishing is a side-line, but a profitable one; lobsters and haddock and saithe abound. Kirkwall is the centre, a thriving town with an airport and the most northerly cathedral in the British Isles.

THE ISLE OF STAFFA

Water colour by Copley Fielding, 1787-1855

SCOÓR EIG, ISLE OF EIG
Coloured aquatint by William Daniell
From Richard Ayton's *A Voyage Round Great Britain*, 1813

North Ronaldshay, visible from Fair Isle, is the most northern of the group, but is said to be "the garden of Orkney." A plane service—one of many in the Scottish Isles—has made it only a twenty-minute journey from Kirkwall, where before it took a day or so by boat. The island is low and protected from the sea by a dry wall made out of the large flat beach rock. The islanders split and dress this rock into huge roof tiles for house and byre, filling the joints with cement and making a coping of straw held down with plaits to cover the roof ridge. Heavy driftwood couples and ties are necessary to support the great weight of these tiles, and the roof must not be steeply pitched. There is a peculiar small short-tailed breed of sheep living between the wall and the sea on North Ronaldshay. It is descended from the wild sheep of the Norsemen and has been banished so long from the island pasture that it is able to live and thrive on seaweed only. In fact the islanders say that it will die if put on a grass diet entirely. The meat, dark and rich in iodine, is consumed locally. Each farmer runs a portion of this flock of about 2,000 beach sheep. At one time the kelp-burning industry threatened the existence of the flock by the excessive cutting of the "tang," but kelp fires no longer burn in the Isles, and instead the sheep find shelter in the remains of the kilns along the wind-swept shore.

On other islands of Scotland small Viking sheep still survive, but their uniformity has been spoilt by outcrossing with Blackfaces and other heavy types. On Soay, St. Kilda, however, there exists a pure type carrying a short dark brown wool prettily marked with cream face-stripes and belly and rump. Some of these Soay sheep are represented in zoological collections. The Pembrokeshire Bird Protection Society has established small flocks on some of its island Nature Reserves.

ISLANDS ROUND IRELAND

SYNGE'S work and the film *Man of Aran* have popularised only one small group of the Irish Islands. Occasionally one hears of the people of Rathlin, nearest Irish island to Scotland, being cut off from the mainland by winter gales for a few weeks, but on the whole little is known of the hundreds of small islands which lie scattered round the north and west coasts of Ireland.

Only a few exist off the east side, and one of the loveliest of these is within an hour's swift sail to the north of Dublin—Lambay, in the possession of the Revelstoke family. Protected from the westerly gales by the east shore of Ireland, it is guarded from the east winds blowing over the Irish Sea by a high hill. It tapers from this hill westwards to a green fertile plain surrounding the harbour. Lambay Castle, restored by Lutyens, stands on a slope gracious and friendly with gardens and woods planned by Gertrude Jekyll. For 350 years it belonged to the Archbishops of Dublin.

Its falcons were sent to the English court. In 1810 there were over one hundred inhabitants living in semi-feudal conditions and much land under the plough. To-day its 600 acres are occupied by one large farm which specialises in early market garden produce, flowers, fruit, sheep, cattle and poultry. Maize and tobacco grow well in the mild sunny and fairly dry climate. The Revelstokes have established a wood of trees of many kinds; the mulberry avenue is one of the finest. The rough hill to the east is railed off as a natural sanctuary for wild life. Here the high cliffs and tumbled shore is the breeding ground of over 60,000 sea-birds of eleven principal kinds. The moorland and heather-covered hill has sheep and cattle and brown and black fallow deer. Altogether a paradise for the lucky owner.

The Saltee Islands, lying off the south-east corner of Ireland, should be made into a bird sanctuary by the Eire authorities. The solitary farm has long been derelict, leaving only the rats to tenant the roofless buildings. Each year sea-birds enlarge their territories there. The latest newcomers are the gannet and fulmar petrel.

South and west there is no island of consequence until we come to Clear Island, with its high Cape a well-known landfall for trans-ocean ships. It is a large island of winding stone-banked lanes covered with gorse and fuchsia. It has several hamlets or small villages, and is inhabited by Irish-speaking crofters and fishermen, and more donkeys than usual—for Ireland. Its climate is probably the mildest in the British Isles. The islanders live simply, like most of the small isles men, on potatoes, milk and eggs. Their exports consist of cattle, donkeys, goats, men and Irish. Of recent years their income has been supplemented by visitors, especially students and Eire Government officials seeking to learn the pure Irish Gaelic as spoken in this remote island. Special leave is now granted to these students to stay on Clear Island for the purpose, and there is more than one inn catering for these aspirants. Here, over a drink of porter, so popular in the west, the latest Irish political news is fiercely or humorously discussed in Gaelic by the young people, or expression is given to the wild Irish gaiety by dancing to the reedy notes of the accordion and the home-built fiddle. Or you can stay in any of the larger thatched cottages which are the farm-houses on this delightful island. There, on a clean linen cloth, will be spread for you hot mealy potatoes, which you peel and eat with your hands, to be followed by a glass of milk—it is this diet, with eggs and fish, which has built the great frames and splendid physique of the men of the west.

Some of the little fields are only thirty yards square; they contain cattle, donkeys, goats, wheat (for home-grown bread), oats, potatoes, seed hay, and cabbages. Seaweed for manure is got from the shore to supplement the home-produced straw dung. On fine days you can go fishing for lobster, crab, crayfish, mackerel, pollack and wrasse; or by night lie off the Fastnet lighthouse in a Cape sailing-smack and set deep lines for giant blackfish. There are several remains of forts and watch-towers on Clear Island,

DOON POINT, RATHLIN
Water colour by A. Nicholl engraved by S. G. Hughes, 1835

including the romantic looking Golden Fort, a castellated ruin on a rocky peninsula. From Cape Clear north along the whole of the west of Ireland we are in a perfect paradise of islands, almost as numerous but not so outflung as the Hebrides. The would-be islander has many to choose from, inhabited and uninhabited. They are most of them exposed to the furious westerly gales which bring the salt and spume-laden seas crashing on their broken cliffs and rolling into the shelter of Bantry and Dingle Bays, the Kenmare River, and Galway Bay. Only in sheltered hollows is the vegetation luxurious. But a summer spent wandering from island to island is a summer never to be forgotten.

The outer inhabited islands have a special interest for, as in Clear Island, the Irish spoken there is now much cherished by "the Dublin creatures" as the Government is sometimes called in the west. In these islands too may be found the last home of the curragh, the light-framed canvas-covered canoe descended from the skin-covered withy frame of primitive man. Various types of curragh are made to-day, ranging from the

43

short squat one-man curragh of Tory Island, to the long gracefully built four-man curraghs of Dingle and the Blaskets. The curragh is a narrow cranky-looking craft, but in the hands of the men of the west it assumes a utilitarian beauty and dignity all its own. Its chief advantages are the ease with which it can be manoeuvred, and its featherweight which enables the islander to land anywhere on rock or sand and carry his boat to safety above the tide-line. The high bow and stern of the curragh enable it to ride a high surf breaking on a flat beach.

These advantages are partly lost in the canoes of Dursey Island, which are built of planks like an ordinary boat and are too heavy to be carried by their crews only. Dursey is an island of hard rock and perhaps the canvas-covered canoe was found to be too flimsy. But the Blaskets are also rock-bound and nowhere is the Dingle curragh more popular than at Great Blasket.

The little farms of Dursey lie on the long south slope of the island. Their fields are warm and early. The crops are in and out of the ground a month earlier than those of the mainland. On the hill ridge above there is summer pasture for sheep and kine. On Dursey dwell a few hardy families who give the visitor who walks the one long lane from east to west a warm welcome, and as in so many island homes here, they talk much of their kin who have "taken the west road," that is to say, who have emigrated to America. Many dollars are sent to the old home on the island by the prosperous emigrants, and not a few of the wanderers answer the call to end their days in the windswept sunlit place of their birth. You hear American accents mingling with the Irish brogue.

The Bull Rock stands to the west of Dursey, facing with a white wall of gannets to the open sea, which has channelled a cave right through the

44

base of the rock. The white tower of a lighthouse crowns the top, giving the rock the appearance of an illustration from a fairy tale. Near by is the Cow, a grassy plateau inhabited by wild birds; and the Calf, a rock subject to immersion in heavy weather, with the lower half of a lighthouse standing as a monument to the tenacity of man in attempting to build securely on a poor foundation.

Far to the north-west are the isolated conical spires of the Skelligs: Little Skellig famous for the world's largest one-site gannet colony (St. Kilda with 17,000 pairs of gannets has three sites) containing 9,500 pairs covering every ledge and foothold of its jagged face; and Great Skellig or Skellig Michael, with its lighthouse and the remains of the monastery of St. Michael. The last consist of some beautifully built stone beehive-type cells, two oratories, some inscribed stones, the chapel and burial ground. There are two fresh-water wells. In this retreat, as we have seen in so many small islands described here, dwelt an early martyr, living what we call to-day the escapist life, away from human contacts, praying for his soul and the souls of all the world. Now the lighthouse-keepers' goats roam over the thrift and sea-flowers which cover the stony cemetery and the monks' garden, and only at rare intervals, so difficult is it to reach the island, do the curious or devout pay tribute with a coin, a flower or a bead laid on the altar of the chapel.

If you climb to the watch-tower—one of many Napoleonic towers which are a distinctive feature of the Irish coast—on the crest of Great Blasket Island you will see the Skelligs, white with sea-birds, standing like two clipper ships becalmed in full sail on the edge of the southern horizon. Maurice O'Sullivan, author of *Twenty Years Agrowing*, stood on this height, talking to his uncle of the days when the Blasket Islanders collected gannets from the Skelligs. O'Sullivan's enchanting book is the best of three produced by Blasket men and women, the others, one by Peg Saiers and one by Tomas O'Crohan, being close seconds for raciness and faithful description. Many of the older Blasket people have no English.

The village of Great Blasket crouches under the hill facing the mainland at Dunquin and Mount Eagle. It is a collection of twenty-four occupied cottages and many more that are derelict. Thatch has been superseded by tarred canvas and laths laid on much as a curragh is built to-day. Life goes easily in these simple two-roomed homes, where a livelihood is obtained from the lobster-fishery, plus a few sheep, a cow or two, and the little fields of oats, barley and potatoes. Peat is cut at the back of the mountain. What more could a man want? There is time to sit in the sun and plan the day, or put off until to-morrow if the sea is rough or the mood unsuitable. This is the good life indeed, with plenty of potatoes, milk, fish, and now and then some sea-birds' eggs or a leg of mutton or lamb. Yet, in spite of these things, in spite of remittances from America, in spite of the summer trade in visitors who wish to learn Irish, or who want to see the background for the tales of the island authors, the resident population dwindles each year.

The off-islets of the Blaskets have their special charm. Inishvickillaun, now uninhabited, was recently the home of the Daly or O'Dala family, fishermen, farmers, violin-makers, and curragh-builders. It is a neat little island large enough to contain a complete farm, fertile in spite of its rocky nature, with little stone-walled fields, a small house after the Blasket fashion, a garden with flowers and vegetables, a small chapel or oratory, plenty of turf for fuel, plenty of rough grazing for sheep, a good anchorage in fine weather, a convenient landing-place for canoes, and the best lobster-fishing in the west of Ireland. Here I have spent many happy days talking to Padrig, last of the O'Dala's to be born on Inishvickillaun, while he made oars and built a violin between the fishing tides.

Inishtooskert also held a farm within living memory. The habitation is built beehive-type, of unmortared stones, partly sunk into the ground, and is still in good condition. All these small islands abound in fulmar and storm-petrels and other sea-birds, and seals.

Next, to the north of the Blaskets and lying off Galway Bay, the Aran Islands have been brought into the public eye through several books, plays and films dealing with the lives of the farmer-fishermen of this wild rocky chain. A steamer covers the thirty miles between Galway and the main island of Inishmore. Much of the arable land has been manufactured, that is, the limestone rock has been overlaid with sand and seaweed and dead vegetation, but if the summer be wet, good crops of potatoes are grown. The little Connemara horses and donkeys thrive, and so do sheep and cattle, for the thin soil is well supplied with calcium from the limestone foundation. But there is no peat, which must be imported at heavy expense from the mainland. The poorer islanders use furze, brambles, driftwood, and cow-dung, "pats" of which are flung against walls to dry. The young boys still wear the kilt or skirt, wool is spun for clothing of all kinds, cowhide pam-pooties are worn on the feet, and the houses are roofed with thatch.

Off Mayo lie the inhabited Clare Island, Inishturk and Inishbofin. Clare is a wet peaty island containing a mountain fifteen hundred feet high, with smaller hills, valleys, streams and trees. It was the home of Grace O'Malley, a vigorous clanswoman who proclaimed herself to be greater than her contemporary Queen Elizabeth. Grace was "powerful in galleys and seamen." She married twice, in each case seizing her husband's castles and dismissing him when she had confirmed herself in possession. She kept her fleet in the splendid natural harbour of Inishbofin, and disposed her boats and galleys about the numerous small islands of this attractive group with such skill that no passing ships escaped payment or dared at-tempt to avoid the toll she claimed for right of passage between Galway and Achil Head. To-day the fishermen-farmers of these islands are peaceful and fairly prosperous, the land being fertile.

DUN AENGUS IN THE ISLE OF ARAN
Engraving, 1795

English is much spoken in this group, but in Tory Island, isolated off the north-west of Donegal, Irish is again the rule and English almost unknown. This is one of the most primitive inhabited islands round Britain, and, as in the Out Skerries of Shetland, much of the landwork is done by hand with rude implements. The harvest is gathered with sickle and sledge. Corn is threshed with hand-flails and winnowed in the wind with a hand sieve.

* * *

The picture presented in this book of the present state of the smaller islands round Britain shows them in a state of change: dwindling and disappearing populations, conversions to nature reserves and sea-bird sanctuaries, and in a few cases the playground of the rich or whimsical. But the day is very near when transport by sea and air will become much easier, and then the most inaccessible island will become habitable. Landings will be made by helicopter and gyroscopic plane where a full-size airfield is not possible. That will be a new era for the little islands. It is well that those who love small islands should consider and plan their proper development for the

best use of the nation, in good time. That planning must take into considera-
tion the retention of the grand natural beauty and amenities of the
small islands. And the fisherman-crofter must be assisted in his struggle
to live an economically successful and decent social life. The men of
his breed manned the navies that saved Britain in her
gravest hours, and they and their islands are to-day a
cherished heritage which needs saving in its turn.

Scudding home

A SHORT BIBLIOGRAPHY

Donald Monro : *Description of the Western Islands of Scotland*, 1818

M. Martin : *A late Voyage to St. Kilda*, 1698

J. H. Gurney : *The Gannet*, 1913

W. Daniell : *A Voyage Round Great Britain*, 1814-25

T. H. Mason : *The Islands of Ireland*, 1936

Hugh MacDiarmid : *The Islands of Scotland*, 1939

Jessie Mothersole : *The Isles of Scilly*, 1910

R. M. Lockley : *I Know An Island*, 1938

F. Fraser Darling : *Island Years*, 1940

Malcolm Stewart : *Ronay*, 1935

Maurice O'Sullivan : *Twenty Years Agrowing*, 1933

John Dickson : *The Islands of the Forth*, 1899